CW00683763

SELECTED POEMS

Also by E.J. Scovell from Carcanet

Collected Poems

E·J·SCOVELL

Selected Poems

CARCANET

First published in 1991 by
Carcanet Press Limited
208-212 Corn Exchange Buildings
Manchester M4 3BQ

Copyright © 1991 E.J. Scovell
The right of E.J. Scovell to be identified as the
author of this work has been asserted by her in
accordance with the Copyright, Designs and Patents
Act of 1988.
All rights reserved

Acknowledgement is made to the editors of *PN Review*,
in which the poems in section X were first published.

British Library Cataloguing in Publication Data
Scovell, E.J. *1907-*
Selected poems.
I. Title
821.914

ISBN 0 85635 922 4

The publisher acknowledges financial assistance from
the Arts Council of Great Britain

Set in 10pt Palatino by Bryan Williamson, Darwen
Printed and bound in England by SRP Ltd, Exeter

Contents

I

II

Light the Fire

Light the fire when night is near,
A little flame to span the night.
He will not feel the winds of fear
In the curved glades of fire-light.

And sing smoothly if you sing,
Lest he should hear between the stresses
The insensible cold rain falling
In unpeopled wildernesses.

With your song and vaulted light
Build his brittle starless ark.
With a curtain on the night
Overthrow the wild and dark.

Fragility of Dusk

The world is stretched so taut and thin
Before the pomps of night begin.
Rain in the air hangs caught like fire,
And every sound a narrow wire
Plucked by fingers out of sight;
And the sky empty, thinned of light;
And night falls crisply flake by flake.
The world is made of stuff so rare,
I think each moment it might break
To dust and vanish in the air
Or, seasoned wood, too dry, might leap
To sudden flame then fall asleep.

Past Time

You'll never understand *No Road This Way*,
But like a lost bird, on the window pane
Beating for skies, you'll throw yourself again
On the glass daylight of departed day.
For there seems open country: "There," you'll say
"The high streams flow between the sky and plain,
Between the hills so bright with hanging rain
The sky's thin atoms are less clear than they."
But light of yesterday is cold like glass.
Time that is past harder than diamond
Turns the fine air, and freezes to the bone.
The sap stirs once and slumbers when we pass.
The breath we breathe just thaws the air beyond,
Till stone we waked returns to harder stone.

Lying Awake

"What have I to do with you?" Sleep said
To one who prayed her come, come to his bed.
"You have desired and lain with Consciousness instead."

To the Ruins by Night

When we came near the ruins I was afraid and lonely.
I told you so, but laughing, to disarm
Fear by a game of fear. You were young only
And might have mocked me, but you took my arm

And stumbling on twigs sprung low in the wet grass
And lost at times in undergrowth and shadows
You brought me to the open, to a star-lit space,
And we saw the abbey near, set in its meadows.

10

You were excited, shining like the sky,
But on my hand your hand was null and light.
Like a leaf I might be carrying I felt it lie
And might have dropped it like a leaf without thought in the night,

And dared not come, though you were set to show me
How quiet the aisles lay in the harmless air.
But I was afraid, because you did not know me,
That if I saw the ghosts you would not be there.

Sand and Light

Every day that the sun sends
The flush will darken on the sands of pearl,
Every night till the world ends
At a known hour the known blue will flood all.

We who find the world is strange,
Come to each moment new as a new lover,
Who are trees to bud and change
Or men to traffic, sailing the seas over,

Their unchanging intercourse,
Day coming to the mineral earth, we never
Dream: for us is steadfastness
Forty years: a thousand years, for ever.

The Candle

Self-complete, unspoken
Single word of flame,
Clear as the unbroken,
The perfect word, the name:
If I try by breaking
Many words to make
Out of all one name
For this single flame,
Mine is not the same.

11

Love, you are your own speech,
You are a word once said
And lifted out of reach
Once in a language dead;
Formed like a crystal, one,
For ever said and done.
In vain with breath you buy
Life's multiplicity
To name that unity.

The Summer Evening

The sun is gone out, the day burnt down.
Now waxen and moth-white
The evening lifts to sight
A cold, extinguished candle's light.

Deep in this light, in this true hour
Is laid away
(In the wax the candle's ray)
All the inflammable substance of day.

It is for this the ox-eyed flowers,
Those that were sparse
In their groups peopling the long grass,
Now are a sea with skies held in their glass.

For this moths only, dense as clay,
And bats with falling flight
Pack the extreme twilight.
On this plumb-line earth drops in night.

The Suicide

Not daylight and not the dark,
Not even the outdoor evening, ebbing,
Yielded this woman her despair,
Her dead she sought, her drowned and still.
Daylight confuses with strong scent.
Darkness is an open door.
Evening is dense with words and tears.

With words we betray the vision.
Words with wind disturb the air,
With breath and eye-bright flicker of wings
Between our sight and still despair.
And tears breed pity, pity is
A tune, and music raises comfort,
The old, starved, elastic moon.

With her face reared, with her stone bows
She parted left and right through streets
The men like clouds. All things she saw
Her seeing mowed and bound in sheaves.
Yet she was quiet as a mouse
Or a small knife that makes its house,
Whose burrow is its own neat size.

And seeing all, she looked beyond
Famished to come to her despair,
And prayed in fear, in rage of will:
"Show me sorrow in still air.
For when I say I am betrayed
Wonder or pain confuses me,
Or a star falls and calls my eyes."

In still air, her own room was
Like an unlidded consciousness,
No light seen there, but a deep-sea,
Pearl-equal visibility.
In that pool she looked and saw,
Image of truth, the essence sorrow;
In that mirror ran to death.

13

The Boy Fishing

I am cold and alone,
On my tree-root sitting as still as stone.
The fish come to my net. I scorned the sun,
The voices on the road, and they have gone.
My eyes are buried in the cold pond, under
The cold, spread leaves; my thoughts are silver-wet.
I have ten stickleback, a half-day's plunder,
Safe in my jar. I shall have ten more yet.

Children's Names

Deep their obscurity,
Unchristened infancy,
Closed being, with no name;
Still, when a name is said,
They are flowers in darkness fed,
Nourished in the shadow of fame.

The names of children are
Name of a distant star,
Of a bird, sealed in green;
Given like a little boat
Vague over waves to float,
Drift light on worlds unseen.

Weak name that cannot bind
These hidden, undefined,
Even in deed not known.
Deeds of men burnish bright
Their name in mortal sight:
These escape, thistledown.

Born Outcast

Born outcast or cast out young,
You famish to return, and lo,
Your feet and hands are home among
Your own; your face is seen to go
Between the native people to and fro.

Your house is in the settlement.
Your little slender tribe's good will
Under the sky first reared your tent –
Which has grown wings of stone, and cast them, till
You need a mountain palace for your pillow.

You need the honour of the stars. You know
You are so poor, you must have all: no less
Will staunch the lesion of the spirit flowing
Ever out into the wilderness
Where you have been, where you are, and are going.

The Giraffe

For neck, a tulip-stalk;
Flower-head, far off and elegant;
Tongue, to fill your body's want
Stretched out like hands of a lady
Who takes her own naturally;
Wind netted in your small-paced walk;

Eyes dark and innocent;
Airy beast with flower's grace,
With bird's speed, with human face;
Painted like ground under trees
With light and shade; supple as these;
Horizon's instrument:

Strength flowers, speed, in you.
Speed is your soul's obedience.
Tiger and strolling wolf must dance
To other tunes, obeying God.
Strength is their fruit, who feed on blood;
But the trees kneel for you.

O meshed among high leaves,
Among clouds: I should never start
To see, when clouds or branches part,
Like a wild cherub's, bloom your head,
Serpent wise, dove feathers spread
Brushing the poplar's sleeves.

A Winter Scene

This is heaven, the winter park they walk in,
Dissolution over, stars with leaves fallen,
The year corrupted away: it is full winter.

Father, child and mother walk in heaven,
Soberly in the mist, the tranquil heart
Of winter, arms linked or hands fallen coldly.

The ragged children are voices glancing on the trees
On the outskirts of heaven. They are heroic foot-prints
On the sodden steep slopes, the mouldered beech-leaves.

The lovers sway clasped hands, walk apart, are silent.
Like travellers on a frieze, like sojourners in heaven
They have forgotten even that they have forgotten.

In a Wood

I saw my love, younger than primroses,
Sleeping in a wood.
Why do I love best what sleep uncloses,
Sorrowful creaturehood?

Dark, labyrinthine with anxiety,
His face is like coiled infancy;
Like parched and wrinkled buds, the first of the year,
Thrown out on winter air.

Stiller than close eyes of a nested bird,
Clear from the covert of his sleeping,
One looked out that knows no human word
But gives me love and weeping.

Death from Cancer

Her face, though smaller than a child's, smaller than a flower,
Seemed forged in iron, or seemed quarried from granite,
Or carved in one stroke by lightning entering
The dense heart of a tree.

Her body had grown small as suddenly
And strangely as a dream dissolved in morning.
Crying through blankets, it seemed to those who had known her
    a woman
Not perished but returned to infancy.

And her skin was delicate and lustreless as woodsorrel,
As moths at dusk; but the east and age in its colour:
And not childhood, not lightness, not springing, but all
Close, compact substance was expressed in her.

Gentle and salt in life: black courage
Unwilled as the pain, and losing war without truce
Remained for her; for them visions of rock uncovered
By the tides of her comfort going down.

17

Bank Holiday: Primrose Hill

On this, the first Bank Holiday
Of the laborious year,
Such gentleness is manifest
In human shapes, in rainy air
Darkening – to make all clear
Man and woman need not speak.

But children's voices on the hill
Searching, answering, swing out far.
One, over space uncreated,
Hangs in the evening like a star,
Star-like rocket ripe for breaking –
Quenched now, swooping in what air?

Eyes at Night

Flowers quicken in the city night:
Their stillness, eyes' activity.
They seem beneath electric light
To look on all things equally
With bold and open innocence.

Eyes that receive and do not speak,
Of flowers, or children late awake;
Gates set too wide, to which worlds flow –
Who sifts that vast intelligence?
Who looks from you? Who sees? I know
In all that comes to thought or sense
The angel of the Judgement Day.

II

The Canal

The canal lies through the city,
Half secretly, indifferently,
Visible and from strangeness invisible.
On other levels, in other worlds

The streets are. Here between the road bridge
Walled breast-high, and railway bridge,
A little shadowed length lies
Of well-deep water bare to sky.

And from one bridge's dark to the other
An empty barge with bright coal-dust lined
Slides smoothly like a fish, silently is
Under the day's eye and his who sees:

As lives of children and thoughts of men glide
In darkness, in the deep, and are on the wave
Lit for moments unannounced,
And those who are there may see.

The Swan's Feet

Who is this whose feet
Close on the water,
Like muscled leaves darker than ivy
Blown back and curved by unwearying wind?
They, that thrust back the water,
Softly crumple now and close, stream in his wake.

These dank weeds are also
Part and plumage of the magnolia-flowering swan.
He puts forth these too –
Leaves of ridged and bitter ivy
Sooted in towns, coal-bright with rain.

21

He is not moved by winds in air
Like the vain boats on the lake.
Lest you think him too a flower of parchment,
Scentless magnolia,
See his living feet under the water fanning.
In the leaves' self blows the efficient wind
That opens and bends closed those leaves.

The Ghosts

The days of our ghosthood were these:
When we were children, when we had no keys
We entered through closed doors, unseen went out again.
Our souls were the dissolved, ungathered, filtering rain.
Our bodies sat upon our parents' knees.

In the second days of our ghosthood
We went on foot among a multitude,
In time of drought, in our hard youth, we winter-born.
And those were visible to men as flowers in corn
Whose souls were eyes unseen that gaze from dark.

We entered flesh and took our veil, our state.
The third days of our ghosthood wait.
When we are stripped by pain, by coming death far-seen,
Of earthly loves, earth's fruit, that came so late to hand,
With that waking or falling into dream
We shall not cross into an unfamiliar land.

Ash Trees

The ash trees grow like fountains
With pliant jets, arched and descending,
And leaves of water many-fingered,
Now by autumn rarefied.

They are blown back upon themselves in wind
Like fountains, and blown wide,
And lose some substance in the air
Beyond their fountain-bowl and sphere,
But most call in, call home.

But where the lost goes no thought follows,
The leaves, the invisible foam struck separate as worlds in air,
In autumn when the substance rends and loosens
And the spirit is pouring everywhere.

A Stranger

I saw a woman drag her foot,
Inept pass through the day,
As if she had an idiot child
Who bled her life away;

As if her ghost stayed in a room
High under roofs, that none
Could see inside; there nursed a fire
That never must burn down.

There like a piled fire intense
Or tree fed by her will,
One lived, unique, a gulf of life
Her life flowed out to fill.

The running children in poor streets
Grazed with their eyes her own.
Far in the mountains of her heart
The infertile streams poured down.

Whom all could wound, yet none could touch,
What child or thought or soul,
Terror or pain she tended there
Her passing did not tell.

An Old Land

Sometimes the mist parts and
The country of your mind appears:
The slow-sloped stubborn hills
And, guessed between, the ferny woods
Like the small shadows in the throats of flowers;

Faithful rocks, and lower
The breathing fields that pray to light;
Few flowers, and some strange, imported,
Run wild. It is an old land, crossed and ploughed and haunted,
And the new year, the present, the eternal,
Lies deep on it like dew.

The Clean Pillow-Case

They gave me a clean alpine pillow-case
And bathed my eyes with snow.
I thought I would not wish for happiness,
For vital joy and energy again –
Release from pain so bears
Its own uncoloured, mountain-scented flowers.

Pain was almost my friend, my hands, my groove,
My part of winter's day.
All the joy I could bear, all I could love
Was innocence and lightness of pain gone,
And in the window's frame
The white air present as a face and name.

Alone

Nothing will fill the salt caves our youth wore:
Happiness later nor a house with corn
Ripe to its walls and open door.
We filtered through to sky and flowed into
A pit full of stars; so we are each alone.
Even in this being alone I meet with you.

A Room at Nightfall

As England's earth moves into dark, the fire is painted,
Shines like speech in the dulled room.
Nocturnal lights of man come out in streets and windows
And cars heard passing. Last to bloom
Of all lights, the narcissus-white lamp on our table
Flowers at a touch, is shaken wide;
And far the sky, Eurydice, falls back, the house-roofs,
Night trees are emptied. We inside
Seem to hang in a domed pearl where light with shadow,
Shadow is interfused with light.
Draw the curtains, perfect the moon-round, moon-coloured
Globe that hangs so still in night.

A Betrothal

Put your hand on my heart, say that you love me as
The woods upon the hills cleave to the hills' contours.

I will uphold you, trunk and shoot and flowering sheaf,
And I will hold you, root and fruit and fallen leaf.

Orchids in a Drought

Wild purple orchids here and there
An inch high in the short grass stood,
As dense with light as precious stones,
As strange on earth as drops of blood:

Stones that have poured and poured their close
Packed colour endless years through earth;
Blood that, deeply lodged in flesh,
Fearful and lustrous comes to birth.

By a dry ditch the dock and rushes,
The buttercup and cowslip head
Hardly looked out over the starved world's roof-top.
Here a deep vein was pricked and bled.

A Wife

Beloved, a year has gone
Whose time seemed still as water of canals.
I am not used to the house linen yet,
The sheets still folded clouds; your china still
On the top shelf shows faces new to me;
And I am still a stranger and
The youngest in your house.

I was born here a second time, to learn
Slowly like a child, by heart and touch,
Till your life's web and furnishing
Grows older in me than my cradle, rooms
Never unknown; till your traits sound
Deeper in me than my inheritance
From childhood and my parents' unplacated genes.

I have drunk forgetfulness
Of former worlds: this is my sole one. Strange
Is to a child one with familiar; but his hands
Dream floating, then are clumsy as they learn

To hold a spoon and button shoes.
Like a long-sleeping child, half by passivity
I learn your substance and soul's reach
As coasts must learn the sea.

The Owl

All night the hunting owls
Above suburban lawns
Answered each other's oboe voices.
O dedicated, limpid wildness!

One stayed self-echoing late
In mindless genius free
When the night was lifted somewhat,
Stretched high and vague above the city,

And day had drawn back far
To spring, fall in song-foam,
Though no birds of day sang yet.
The owl called on and on alone,

All space its sheath and ear;
Then ceased and nothing was.
Suddenly – what wild valley crossed? –
A blackbird's voice of friend spoke near.

Time for Sleeping.

Do not look up. I will turn away soon.
The light is trained down on your book; your head
Shows lit yet, incandescent as the moon
Seems. What is still between us is not dead;

It sleeps and draws far in itself in dreams.
My thought and gazing, like a willow leaf,
Shallowly comb that deep; the surface gleams
Frayed now. My greedy consciousness and grief

Confused and anxious cry to love to wake,
To know itself each hour because life flies.
I think of war and death. You, for life's sake,
In our love's time for sleeping do not raise your eyes.

Day and Night

My life drains down to sleep.
The dayward slopes are dry and wear
A desert beauty only,
Unploughed and full of air,
And the air full of light, and colour unborn.

There the short grasses vowed
To poverty and namelessness
Make themselves into seas to mirror sky,
And wide-spaced sheep feed on the grass,
And seem grown thin, fed on eternity.

But the dark slopes tax
My dole of life with storms and streams.
Adult-born rivers spring from the divide
Of falling asleep, and breed rankness of dreams,
Hang the exhausting creepers in the glades.

And voices sip my blood.
It is my dream-selves and their friends
Using my life because they must
For their strong, trivial ends,
To throw me out on morning bleached and drowned.

III   *Poems on Infancy*

The First Year

I

All deeds undone, all words unsaid,
Null as a flower, sleep on my bed.
None to compare you with, for you
Are type and inmost form of New.

Darkness your home — what need at all
To be cast out, washed, wrapped in shawl;
And soon, the same yet not the same,
Be bent to attributes and name?

What should you do, new born, but fall
Asleep, in sleep disclosing all?
What can you do but sleep, an hour from birth,
Lacking an answer yet to give to earth?

II

Before she first had smiled or looked with calm
Light-answering eyes and claimed to be of man
I put my finger in her shadowy palm,
And her own whispering ones from their chestnut fan
Closed again (as they must) on mine, to a bud.
Then I was where strong currents piled and slackened.
Like a pulse telling all the power of blood
This palm seemed the cavern where alone her darkened
And secret rock-roofed river showed to man
(Except when one inside half-raised the blind
Of her inky eyes, and fierce a dark beam ran
Searchlighting day). So I strayed on her mind;
And thought I trespassed in that covered land.
Her hand seemed private, still an unborn hand.

III

In what dignity she lies
Resting on her world
Her unjudging, cloudless eyes;

Making helplessness protection;
Making immaturity
(So full she fills her state) perfection.

Perfectly, without room for more or less,
Her unskilled body arches to express
To a known face coming, joy and friendliness.

IV

Is it then an imaginary world
Where I speak to my baby in English words,
And half believe she understands my tongue
Like the young of animals and birds;
Half think we play a game she understands,
And she laughs at being a child, weak in my hands?

V

As monks whose time is told by bells
Out of their strict hours see eternity,
I have watched your eternity, your world without beginning,
These five months by the moon;

These days by the clock with their ritual repetitions,
Votive milk and early rising,
Plains of peace and fainting terrors,
And their meaning out of time.

For between one feed and another,
Your sleep's forgetting, your calms of waking
Have freed me to eternity
Like the sky through a little window-frame.

VI

I am absorbed and clouded by a sensual love
Of one whose soul is sense and flesh the substance of
Her spirit; and her thoughts, like grass shadowed by the wind's
    flight,
Her hands' bemused and under-water dance in light.

Will, waked in lashing limbs, drops in her like a flame.
Her love is parting of lips to suck or smile (whose birth the same);
Her excreting, her lonely task; her communication,
Her body arched for hands to hold, harp-strung with jubilation.

When I serve her (whose sense is soul) I serve her all,
Whose feeding is her love, whose mind in bone grows tall;
And watching her (whose thoughts move without words like
    wind on grass)
I am less than I was my own; I am not what I was.

VII

The days fail: night broods over afternoon:
And at my child's first drink beyond the night
Her skin is silver in the early light.
Sweet the grey morning and the raiders gone.

VIII

The baby in her blue night-jacket, propped on hands
With head raised, coming out to day, has half-way sloughed
The bed-clothes, as a sea-lion, as a mermaid
Half sloughs the sea, rooted in sea, basking on strands.

Like a gentle coastal creature she looks round
At one who comes and goes the far side of her bars;
Firm in her place and lapped by blankets; here like tides
Familiar rise and fall our care for her, our sounds.

IX

Whom do I know? Who learns from me to kiss, to play?
Who answers sound with sound and looks with eyes of friend?
Strange that this long first year of life, this standing day
In which you are set like stone in ring, in which we meet, will
    more than end;

Will drop far out of sight, and you become another,
Sister and stranger to this self, changed without motion,
Caught in acquirements, calling things names, calling me mother;
But lost this lucid year, dropped out of sight, this key dropped
   in the ocean.

X

The child looks out and away: to the woman's maternal-bound
Thought away raying from her, light-reined; but chiefly
She looks away from herself, when on the floor she briefly
With all the moment's life examines a hair-pin found
Or a knot in the board; or when her fingers spell
(Whose gestures are diffident and tender) – touch and trace,
As if they searched there for the features of a face,
The carpet's pattern, never seen before so well.

It does not surprise the baby that she is a human
Soul already, established citizen of earth;
She takes her life and state for granted, teased the most
By little concrete things; but it surprises the woman,
Still seeing her face, formed and reserved, the day of birth,
And the perils and the spaces of her voyage to this green coast.

XI

When the old sleep, a sadness moves beholders;
And when the strong mature, whose shoulders
Support the world in their generation's hour –
Strangely sleep's weakness lies with power;
But when you sleep, sleep only seems your other
Self, your flower's leaf, your brother.

Sleep's unknowing, where so little's known,
Is a lamb with a lamb lying down.
And sleep's imprudence and unguarded nature
You wear like any thornless creature,
Open, upturned to dangerous nights and days
Like scabious where the cattle graze.

Not fast like ours your categories seem;
Your dreams play with your waking dream.
And bold all visions come into your net –
The rage of thought not on you yet,
That frightens the many to a standing stone
So it may seize and have the one.

Not at the pillow end of your big bed
You sleep, but where your wandering head
Happens to tire and rest. So sometimes, thrown
Far out on your blue eiderdown,
You seem a sleeping sea-bird, guarded best
By yielding to the sea, wild sea its friend and nest.

A Moment

The apple blossom, the sensuous infant charm;
The human rounded arm
Dipping to the elbow, with that slight scythe-twist,
The forearm's swerve to wrist;

The bibs and pots and the elaborate care
Round her continuous as air;
Her time of life with all its dress, with its cloud-scapes
Muffling the sky in gleams and shapes;

Her childhood and its circumstance fell far away
Then as she turned from window-play
With a fledged, conscious look. It seemed a bird stretching,
Seven feet from wing to wing.

A Boy of Four Months

In his first flowering, in the prime and pause,
The summer of his infancy,
The dark-blond boy on the strange bed alone
Lies like a rosy stone cast by the sea.

He is as self-sufficient as the stone,
Rounded with milk; and like the air
Or like a dream, a waking calm well-being
Laps him and folds and enters everywhere.

In the simplicity of his receiving
Our world – our feeding, tending and leaving
And looming again (he opens like a flower
To a smile on the bed) – there strongest sleeps his power.

A Baby's Head

The lamp shines on his innocent wild head again.
Only for a moment are you both flowers and men,
Your souls like souls of flowers wholly immanent;
Your soul a texture and your love a scent.

In fifty years if you have beauty it will be
Words written on your face, abstract as history.
The light will call you foreign with its sharp and changed
Glancing, among earth's aspects call you strange.

Now even the captive light still in a sheltered room,
Claiming you as its kind, pours round your head in bloom,
So melting where it flows that the strong, armour-browed
Skull seems as pervious as a cloud;

Or seems a field of corn by the wind liquefied
Streaming over the arches of a round hill-side.
Contours and skin make tender the planes of light and shadow
The pale and darker gold of the upland meadow.

Only for a moment your cavernous human brow
Will dwell in the world of sense as naturally as now,
Beautiful with no meaning, but that it commands
Those to love, who hold you in their hands.

Child Waking

The child sleeps in the daytime,
With his abandoned, with his jetsam look,
On the bare mattress, across the cot's corner;
Covers and toys thrown out, a routine labour.

Relaxed in sleep and light,
Face upwards, never so clear a prey to eyes;
Like a walled town surprised out of the air –
All life called in, yet all laid bare

To the enemy above –
He has taken cover in daylight, gone to ground
In his own short length, his body strong in bleached
Blue cotton and his arms outstretched.

Now he opens eyes but not
To see at first; they reflect the light like snow,
And I wait in doubt if he sleeps or wakes, till I see
Slight pain of effort at the boundary

And hear how the trifling wound
Of bewilderment fetches a caverned cry
As he crosses out of sleep – at once to recover
His place and poise, and smile as I lift him over.

But I recall the blue-
White snowfield of his eyes empty of sight
High between dream and day, and think how there
The soul might rise visible as a flower.

Song for a Young Mother

There, there, you fit my lap
Like an acorn its cup,
Your weight upon my arm
Is like a golden plum,
Like an apple in the hand
Or a stone on the ground.

As a bird in the fallow
Scoops a shallow hollow
Where the earth's upward pressing
Answers egg and nestling
– Earth's mass the beginning
Of all their learning –

So you learn from my arm
You have substance and a home.
So I learn from your birth
That I am not vague and wild
But as solid as my child
And as constant as the earth.

All Children's Beauty

All children's beauty is dear
To me because of you
As yours is for all children's sake.

One crying in park or street,
From misery or beating will,
Plucks across space a note from a nerve tuned by you.

And when you cry, to whom I can run to bring peace,
I think of the unappeasable crying
Of children starved in Poland or in Greece.

Flowers of Almond

Begotten in our war's mid-winter, shoots of faith,
The children spangling early spring seem the cold flowers
Of almond on black twigs like pearls of gum pressed forth.
Children are always strewn on earth, but these are ours,

And we are weak in faith, and we can thwart conceiving.
What pressed these heavenly drops, these stars, from our dark
      branches?
Our own, or all mankind's importunate believing?
On the white sky, in the north wind, how bold their dances.

A Face

Nothing more beautiful will come my way
Than his face tilted where it lay,
Lay as it happened in my elbow's crook
(A child of four), yet with that look
Of lit from farther than the stars. His eyes
Were shut, and other gates likewise
That give on the world, though his nape knew where best,
Rumpling my sleeve, to come to rest;
Then lay in living stillness. Nothing here
But lines by chance handsome, skin clear
As children's is; but meaning with such power
Flowed through, I could have watched an hour;
As on a bridge above a waterfall
We watch one form, through which flows all.

IV

Shadows of Chrysanthemums

Where the flowers lean to their shadows on the wall
The shadow flowers outshine them all,
Answering their wild lightness with a deeper tone
And clearer pattern than their own
(For they are like flames in sun, or saints in trance,
Almost invisible, dissolved in radiance).

But space in that shadow world lengthens, its creatures
Fall back and distance takes their features;
The shadows of the flowers that lean away
Are blurred like milky nebulae;
And faint as though a ghost had risen between
The lamplight and the wall, they seem divined, not seen.

The dying wild chrysanthemums, the white,
Yellow and pink are levelled in light;
But here in their shadows, tones remain, where deep
Is set on deep, and pallors keep
Their far-off stations, and the florets more
Subtly crisp their bright profiles, or are lost in the flower.

An Elegy

In early winter before the first snow
When the earth shows in garden beds
(For the foam is blown of flower-heads
And the gardener has cut low
Or tied in place the stock and green)
When the world wears an inward mien
Of mourning and of deprivation,
The appearance fits this time and nation.

In early winter before the first snow,
The child whose steps began in June
In the short misty afternoon
Walks in the mournful park below

43

Branches of trees, and standing stretches
Her arms and sings her wordless catches.
Like light her play and happiness
Flicker on the world's distress.

In this city still unraided
Where the queues stretch round the corners
It befits us to be mourners
Who read of other lands invaded,
Who have heard at night death pass
To northern cities over us.
It befits us who live on
To consider and to mourn.

The quiet days before the snow,
The child's feet on the yellowing grass –
How can I make a rite of these
To mourn the pang I do not know,
Death fastened on the life of man?
Sorrow uses what it can.
Take as my rite this winter tune:
The child's walk in the darkening afternoon.

Daylight Alert

When the daylight Alert has sounded, calling us
To what? not fear but application – we seem to have stepped
      across
A line in time, like a low wall that nettles guard,
Into a place marked off, an orchard or unkept graveyard.

The long gust sinks to peace, children who cried recover
Their joy; we stand in grass and look, the low wall is crossed
      over.
This is another realm where silence is so loud,
The sky shines so, the grass springs thicker, the fruits rush and
      thud.

44

Bombs have not fallen on our town; the shoppers scarcely
Lift eyes to the clear sky and fighters crossing straight and
    sparsely.
Our blood no more than smiles at this *memento mori*
As if it were a skull in flowers or a pale murder story.

Only our souls say in the stillness of their breath:
This is the hour that may be ours, the hour of pain and death.
What are we waiting for? What are we stretched to meet
Here in a walled and haunted plot set in our shopping street?

The hour shuts like a flower or dream when it is ended,
The far wall come upon too suddenly, the All Clear sounded.
It was not death but life we were called to entertain,
Waving to one who flashed so fast by in a royal train;

Called not to death but thought, still called to application,
Standing with empty eyes, dropped hands, at the small railway
    station,
On the flowered country platform, we who have come so far
To honour one we never meet – wind, is he? Falling star?

A Naturalist

The stones and dust seemed flowers in the lane's warm shade.
He in his dust-white coat went down through the breached
Low wall by the road into a flowering glade
Where the small briars his hand, the cow-parsnip reached
His shoulder, with flower-heads, level umbels spread
On their thick fluted pillars, head beyond head.

Spacing the parsnip flowers and passenger rose,
The grass like air stood everywhere in channels.
There he thigh-deep, a patient man in flannels,
With his glass-green net still, and in repose
His heavy thoughtful head, seemed rooted in the brome,
Stock of that natural garden, never so at home.

The Tree on Christmas Eve

All things that beam like water and like snow
Faceted glance and sparkle cover
The little spruce tree. Frosty rivers flow
Along its branches, weighted over
As if by snow's lax watery load, by clasps
Of candles and hung moons of glass.

A stranger in the room, yet the room's heart
And its cold silver midnight hearth;
Candles unlit, yet streams of light flow out;
The tree one flower, like moonlit earth,
Flower without face, yet does tonight possess
The face's flower and crown of singleness.

A Vapour Trail over the Park

And the families go home
And the ducks stand on the weed,
And the leaves set broad to sun
Have taken all they can.

The baby as the beeches loom
Prints his full face and heavy lids
(By sunlight, like the day, washed pale)
On a dark green deep.

And time might sleep; but vertical
Dropping, slow, invisible,
A plane divides the sky's blue cliff
With a mountain waterfall.

A Refugee

My heart had learnt the habit of earthly life
In an accustomed place.
My voice had learnt the habit of maternal
Sharpness and gentleness.

My thighs had learnt the speech of love. The house
And market tasks that show
So small a flower, rooting in hands and feet
Had matted my flesh through.

My husband died in the mercy of Russian snow.
My child died in the train,
In three days in the weeping cattle truck
From Breslau to Berlin.

I was not taught the song of extremity,
The dancing of duress.
All that I know of infinite is the intensity
Of finite tenderness.

All that I have of goodness is through love –
Their love my only worth.
My rigid arms set in the shape of their love
Have no more use on earth.

A Dark World

Under the pent-house branches the eight swans have come,
Into the black-green water round the roots of the yew;
Like a beam descending the lake, the stairway to their room.

The young swans in their tender smoke-grey feathers, blown
By wind or light to a faint copper smouldering,
Come docile with their parents still, three-quarters grown.

The old swans, built of light like marble, tower and scatter
Light in the dusk; but the young are mate to the yew's shade.
With their dim-green webbed feet like hands they part the water

And wind among its loops and eyes of mercury
Less visible than these they have wakened; and beside
The trellised roots they twine their necks as fine and grey.

In groups and in their fugue following one another
They turn to constant music their intercourse; and passing
With neck stretched on, with greyhound brow, brother by
        brother,

Or slowlier drawing level, where their mute and furled
Wings touch they loose a feather to float on the night-face
Of water, with white stars to drift as a dark world.

The Day of Widowhood

This is the shadow of her weddingtide,
And she again distinguished like a bride.
The shadow falls certain from that day's sun
Since what is done in time must be undone.

Caught in a shaft of darkness, strange her grey
Dim well-deep face lies on the coloured day,
On wind and flowering grass and rain held high,
With trees like rain slanted against the sky.

But her eyes inward turned watch by the bed and tomb
Of her long marriage; by his face in death become
All profile like a mountain range. O height of face,
O earth stamped with unyielding singleness!

Herself again pierced on a height and crowned,
She looks across the lower soft and broken ground
To the first peak of love; and to her view
Her life is simple, hung between these two.

48

Who bore and nursed his children here at length
Has borne him over death, death giving strength;
And vision dwells in her extremity,
Peace in her thought: "This is what was to be."

Though her mouth's weeping tremulous denies
Vision and peace, and though his absence cries
Like a night bird, and though the common seeks to cover,
What is done in eternity will not be grassed over.

After Midsummer

Love, we curve downwards, we are set to night
After our midsummer of longest light,
After hay harvest, though the days are warmer
And fruit is rounding on the lap of summer.

Still as in youth in this time of our fruition
Thought sifts to space through the words of definition,
But strangeness darkens now to a constant mood
Like hands shone dark with use or hafts of wood;

And over our dense days of activity
Brooding like stillness and satiety
The wonder deepens as clouds mass over corn
That here we are wakened and to this world born

That with its few colours so steeps and dyes
Our hearts, and with its runic signs implies
Meaning we doubt we read, yet love and fear
The forms more for the darkened light they bear.

It was so in youth too; now youth's spaces gone
And death of parents and our time's dark tone
Shadow our days – even children too, whose birth
And care through by-ways bring our thoughts to death;

Whose force of life speaks of the distant future,
Their helplessness of helpless animal nature;
Who, like the old in their shroud of age, close bound
In childhood, impress our natural pattern and end.

The springy twigs arch over walls and beds
Of lilac buddleia, and the long flower-heads
Run down the air like valleys. Not by force
But weight, the flowers of summer bend our course;

And whether we live or die, from this time on
We must know death better; though here as we stand upon
The rounded summit we think how softly the slope
And the sky have changed, and the further dales come up.

Evening Scene

The waves lay down their trail,
On the brown water feathers of foam.
Over the dark bituminous sands
The stragglers loiter home.

Where the stream seeps to sea
And the sands are a tarnished glass to the sky
They walk as if on evening light,
They run and seem to fly.

The shallow acre-wide
Waves of low tide swathe their feet like a meadow.
Surely they feel themselves unmade,
Spirits that cast no shadow.

I see them small, distinct,
Dark, and see on the sheen of what wings they fly,
The two lit wings of land and sea,
The one vane of the sky;

And see, not near nor far,
The black-brown cliffs stand with their slopes of green
Stippled with darkness. All of space
Is the sand's width between.

Return from the Beach

Across the sands burdened with their dark tone,
With heat of honey and with seams of stone-
Blue shade under the day-long azure,
The holiday-makers turn from pleasure,

Turn from the brilliant west in twos and fours,
In groups dispersed and quiet, with their powers
Of play before the light failing,
With trailing child and his spade trailing;

The women bearing their weight, the youths their lightness,
The outriding boys still in a mould of brightness,
The girl tranced by beatitude,
The man pleased with his hardihood,

All in their human posture pacing on
As if they carried their lives in the form of a crown.
Late cricketers, a lingering couple
With gulls possess the world of opal.

Michaelmas Summer

Each day we waken to a summer day,
Till the whole summer seems a summer day
That opens on an estuary of evening
Endless, as any summer morning may,

When light seems not to change unless to increase
By the slow settling of its ash of peace.
So in this Michaelmas summer whose days
Are evening hours, which are eternities,

Each day lays down – like bees that one by one
File into time – its apple, aster, sun;
Each day lays down a coal on the slow fire
Of the real season and this miraged one

That seems it cannot end; each day of summer given
Beyond longing, feeds in us the illusion or the vision
Of Heaven on Earth, of Heaven in Heaven.

November Afternoon

The light is a feeble flood over the meadow
But the river under its low bank is in shadow.

The oarsmen wait for the lock to clear
On the tranced water hanging over the weir.

In their white singlets they droop arm and shoulder
And know the passing of time as the air falls colder.

The few pale heart-shaped poplar leaves are bright
Beyond, selected by the searching light.

In November

By rivers and in gardens in this brown November
Between the nameless bird-brown tones of fawn and umber
In fading leaf and fallow stem and open tree
We walk on Earth's transparency,

Through scenes that all as one like curtains sway, that faintly
Doubtfully breathe and sigh like a sleeper watched intently;
Where low skies stretch to infinite the river shores
And formal gardens' corridors

And children play on the sodden grass. The elm-trees' rare
Yellow leaves are subdued as light on their mouse-hair.
They race in childhood's legendary pastures; we
In our habit of maturity

Walk on transparent Earth in autumn sieved with space,
On Earth of light withdrawn and flowering called to base,
And tissue of atoms torn – yet most now, all in jeopardy,
Teacher to us of truth, form of reality.

The Death-Bed

"I died in bed, in age, at home, alone,
Although among my own yet with none known,
In kindness of strangers, strangeness of my kin
Whose votive eyes were turned to death's not mine,
My death so changing them they died for me
To nameless shades of mere humanity.

"Thinner than air, they had no power to keep
My recognition summoned by the deep
Engaging themes of young maturity,
When between forward dream and reverie
Of age, between all guessed-at and all done,
My love and path were found and children born.

"There memory lapsed and roaming, once I said
(Propped in a foreign land on a strange bed)
'This is my wedding day', and saw on their pale
Devoted lips the image of my smile,
Bashful and winning; for no other mirror
They held to me to teach me truth or terror.

"A shade they called my daughter came to me.
I stirred and spoke of my young family
That I must care for: when I would have risen
I felt my weakness and the bed my prison,
Yet thought I should not die, so strangely I seemed then
To have known a later time, awake or dreaming.

"But the dream worn to fragmentary sand
Sounded in sleep; what more I understand
Untellable."
                    The watchers say
"It seemed we died your death, yourself so far away,
Free in your past, in sleep; and yet it was not so.
Forgive us our life and that we let you go."

V

Garden Sonnets

I SINGLE PEONY

Chestnut and holm-oak and the tulip tree
Are shadowers of college lawns, between
Whose walls of stone deeper the drifts of green
Form than in open fields; whose peony
Is redder than wild poppies. Now the dense
And globe-round bud risen compact and close
Breaks to a flowing grace, as hands fall loose.
Yet the red of the flower is a well of reticence.

Flower out of China, though long domiciled
Like the garden trees, keeping as alien mark
Tincture's intensity well-deep and dark:
How it draws eyes with that, where on its field
Of strong and copious mid-green leaves the cup
Lies wide, with yellow stamens lifted up.

II COPPER BEECH

The lights are moonlight on the copper beech,
But for a scattering fall of sun direct
Over one shoulder, single leaves reflect.
This far side where no strays of sun can reach
The leaves are carved by moonlight each from each.
Through dusk of spring their undeciphered colour
Under its shadowing bloom has ripened fuller;
Now night builds like a dove in cleft and breach.

The flowering chestnuts are sunlit and rounded.
I study this dark, delta-branching tree,
Stream flowing to its moonlit estuary
Out of the mountain rocks where it is grounded.
I touch the leaves clammy with honeydew
And trace the veins that the dark blood runs through.

An Old Woman Reflects

My life was a novel read by the fire on a winter
Evening between supper and sleep.
My manner of reading is greedy, blind and deep.
The latch was down, no one could enter.

The story was long, and the elders mid-way died;
The child turned woman, the heat-haze lifted;
And stilly at times, the contours sank or shifted
As when deep tunnellings subside.

And the interest spread through branches, generations –
The tale grown complex, wide and shallow.
Yet most towards the end came (if I follow)
Echoing themes, returning passions.

Little it all may mean; little and all.
For I plunged in it as one may in dreams;
I gave myself, four hours by the clock it seems,
To its truth of dream, to its dream-clear call.

O dreamed, confused, headlong and lingering
Life! Yet all things that came to me
Came, great and small, with such authority
As doves with tokens from a king.

Now I raise my eyes dazzled. The forms, the bright
Voices shred by, die echoing down.
I must return to life. Oh, I must turn
And lift the blind, and read the night.

Light and Flowers

Perfect, opaque – there seemed no way
In, no word for words to say.
Like the white moon clear in the sky by day

The white flowers hung on the blue wall
Distant in beauty, and the fall
Was absolute, no foothold there at all.

But set in the west window soon
As evening crumbles afternoon
And blue and white are merged and overthrown,

Those flowers that seemed only a little
Translucent, less than finest brittle
China, now stream with light through every petal.

Light wakes in them their own shadows,
Bringing them darkness, as it does
All textures it penetrates, water and glass;

And drowns, and lays on its flood-plain –
Filled with the breath of life again –
These that seemed once flowers of porcelain.

Summer Night

The summer night is sea-blue still
Behind the street-lamps to the west and north
And downy seeds of poplar drift
Like gossamer on ankles and on mouth.

In midnight rooms the lagging day
On sheets and blankets leaves flood-pools of white,
That wait like summer sleeplessness
For new day's flow, beyond this feint of night.

A flower is pressed on the window pane:
White poppy, by translucence shadowed blue.
The children sigh in sleep, the hair
At the nape of their neck damp as with honey-dew.

One Wave

At the late end of evening when
Only the white remain
Printed on darkness, of all flowers
– White lilies and campanulas,
The white maroon-spotted foxglove –
And sweet and chilling damp airs move,

There is one moment when the white
Flowers are changed to gulls on night.
For night in waves flows like a sea,
Not imperceptibly.
There is one wave rocks the beached boat,
Lifts, and it is afloat.

A Short Night

She is in the garden weeding almost in darkness.
Indoors we say it is quite dark. Fetch her in.
Soon now the hedges will be filled with mist
At daybreak, in the bird's hour. Get her to come.
Call your wife, our hostess, home.

So she comes in, tranquil, grubby and vague
With gardening, bringing the scent of stock through the door,
Bringing her unbelief in time, with the frailty
Of the phantasmal summer night,
And makes us tea and puts the tray on the floor,
And the talk flourishes more than before.

Two Notes on Parenthood

I   THE WALL

I did not know I was to be
Built into a wall and weathered like a stone
To an anonymous ripeness of tone,
And with valerian and toadflax grown,
And all the future rest on me.

2   THE DIFFIDENT PARENTS

Then grow as plants do, merely grow.
Lightly enough we cannot touch you.
Though in a dream we seem to watch you
Skied on some stage, and we below
Divided by the impalpable lights,
Yet dreams arise only to pass,
And you must live entwined with us
Through years of actual days and nights.
Then be light-footed on the thin
Ice bridge above our deep crevasses.
Find pasture in our wildernesses.
All that we know, have done and been
Distils to a strange milk, and yet
You bless the bowl, drinking from it.

Growing Girl

Watching from the high brick wall
The younger children's tennis in the lane
Her eyes run thoughtless with the ball,
And the coasts of her face rise clear and plain.

Undiscovered or forsaken wholly
Against the sky those slops and dunes lie now,
Moulded in natural melancholy
Of untilled country, chin and cheek and brow.

The hour absorbs the players and the girl
Dreaming above the clematis. The ball
Coming and going weaves its spell,

And her eyes with the ball run to and fro.
Only the tracts of cheek and temple know
She has a long journey to go.

A Kitten's Life

My friend's child had a kitten
Someone had weaned too young. I never heard
How it was brought into the child's possession.

A breath, a condensation
Of underlying vapour to faint cloud,
It seemed less animal than visitation;

Less like a cat than silver-
Smooth deep-sea fish brought strange and dumb to hand;
Fuller of distance than a journeying elver.

And yet its hardly-seeing
Sweet-slanting eyes (as now we understand)
In each direction looked towards not being.

Though it made no demands
They had given it what they could. It lay in wool
A week, touched milk, purred faintly in their hands.

On Mount Olympus wild
Our garden pansies grow, whose eyes recall
– *Viola gracilis* – kitten and child.

King Richard II *at Stratford-on-Avon*

1

Out of a sweetness nothing could increase –
So it must change or fall to less –
The evening landscape, wax to light
Like honey-comb and filled with it;
The ochre stain on dark trees here and there,
The one branch seized with fire,
And autumn daisies amethyst
Common as bonfire smoke or mist;

Out of our slow drive and our halting late
To watch across a pasture gate
The cattle branching from a ground
Of cloud and trees white-flooded round;
Out of our prelude and anticipation
That was itself fruition
We came with night to the white river swans
And white-invested Richard's tones.

2

Wound in his white cloud of imagination
Richard is dead, who had the mind to see
And saw his name a light in history,
Who read the cryptic words of his vocation
And answered dazzled and unluckily,
Wound in the white shroud of his fantasy.

Weakest of all, mere water, changed through watery
Prismatic opal to the shine of snow;
Against the rocks and seething, a bright bow
Blown with sea spray; weaker than flattery,
Subject to words and swords; through dream and show
And iron force falling to lie like snow.

Poet and actor raised this apparition,
A rainbow truth altering for every eye –
Not him who died in real obscurity

Slipping his life of ruin and negation
And left for Shakespeare's finding that *trouvaille*,
As if he had seen his name a light in poetry.

3

He died in real obscurity.
But our King Richard dies
Comforted by poetry
And tears of watching eyes
From century to century.

Here fused is all complexity:
His life; the imputed words;
And that male stride through history
Of heroes with their swords
The actors flash us from the boards.

Real and imagined mingle here
As colours fuse to white,
Or as the rays from everywhere
Converge to form one light
Upon a throne, upon a bier;

Or as the roads and cars flow in
To Stratford, and we come
With light of what we have known and been
To lay upon this tomb;
With evening mist and autumn scene.

Love of the Seashore

We come out of a fern-set lane
To tamarisk on the foreshore and
The grass that binds the blond dune sand
And at the ebb a perfect fan,

A coral shell on the furthest beaches
Cast like a dream and soon to fade,
Fall from its salt and pricking shade;
To gulls glassed on their ice-blue stretches,

And to our gull-like outpost stations –
Pouring on pools and waves in trance,
We who are parents, citizens
From neighbourhoods and occupations.

Love of the seashore, lasting faith
So draws us long past infancy,
Past youth, to cape and estuary;
Image of love of sleep not death;

Not love of death, of that full deep
That sluiced from its horizon pours,
The Atlantic soul, to bury ours;
But tidal dailiness of sleep.

Our failure is around us, wrack,
Spoiled picnic, castle trodden over.
Cover with waves our shallows, cover
And drown our world to give it back.

Sleep, rectifying solitude,
Sleep that attunes our daylight faces,
Brother to free and lonely places
Brings marvels also on its flood.

So, these like dreams, sea-wave and shell,
The green-veined blue, the oxblood stone
Come strange with truth beyond our own,
So far-brought, patterned, beautiful,

Come laden to us margin-lovers
Here where we take in hands and sight
All we can bear of infinite;
Haunters of thresholds, gulls and plovers.

Song for a Ghost

When or where I cannot guess,
I lost my life in the deep grass
Between youth and middle age,
Not with pain and consciousness
But like a brooch dropped from a dress.

Will the search never be over
Through the trampled grass and clover
Between youth and middle age
Where I slept by hedge and river,
Where I dreamed it was for ever?

While we sleep there's life to lose.
Which of all the flowers I choose
Between youth and middle age
Cupped the poison? Or which grass
Soft of blade was honed to pierce?

When or where I cannot guess,
I lost my life in the deep grass
Between youth and middle age,
Not with pain and consciousness
But like a brooch dropped from a dress.

The Vine at Hampton Court

Nothing is in its house but the great vine
And a skein hung of raffia, large to scale,
And high step-ladder propped on the far wall.

Nothing but the vine in its long house,
And the vine grown its house – all but the rock-
Shaped and clay-coloured, swollen, fantastic stock,

From which the dedicated branches run
Piping their roof's length, held against the sky,
Earth to the leaves, that give them back the sun;

Leaves trained to spread to the utmost, tessellate
Themselves their ceiling, even themselves become
The light that inhabits sole their empty room;

Light fair in colour, filling wall to wall.
For now is spring, the grapes hang high and small.
The tender light, the lucent tree are all.

The River Steamer

Waiting for a spirit to trouble the water.

Waiting for a spirit from beneath or over
To trouble the surface of the river
From which the hours like clouds reflected gaze
White, and the daylight shines of all earth's days,

Waiting for a spirit to dissolve the glass,
I see, in the unbreaking wave that fans from us,
Incline and circle the reeds and sedges;
And see the ripples on the under sides of bridges

And under the dark green leaves of deepest summer
And the green awning of the river steamer,
The secondary ripple, the shadow's shadow,
Abstract and pure appearance, follow and follow;

And see the roan banks flecked with rose and seed
Of willow-herb, and fields beside the river-bed
Freshened by total light in day's decline,
And the elms standing in the heart of the sun;

And hear the passengers telling the day's praises,
And the tired wildness of their children's voices
Too young for the journey's hours; and all of these
Clear in the river's glass, I also praise,

Waiting for a spirit to transpierce the glaze.

67

Visit to a Child at Night

Why so still, so wide awake, cold face
And bird-in-bramble eyes coloured with dark's darkness?
The little light, that entering I let in
From distant turns of stair, draws whiteness from your skin
As even moonless nights from waterfalls
And tracts of flood and heart-shaped pools.

Then were you watching night, so quiet I took you
For long asleep, or did my tread on carpet wake you?
Or do your eyes, as black as new-born, blind
Gaze from another night and hemisphere of mind?
If this is sleep I fear to rouse you, speaking.
Speak to me first if this is waking.

Though we seem met by flood or heart-shaped pool,
By less than moonlight or the moon invisible,
Caught to a zone of mysteries and dangers,
It is not for the first time and we are not strangers.
I say your name. Who should it be but I?
Asleep or waking, you reply.

Walking into Yew Woods

The ribbon-leaved grass is in seed
In clearings and by paths, the blade
And loose grain bowed, grace to remember,
Printed on deep or broken shade
Or violet-flowering glades in full September.

But far in the yew wood soil is dry,
Kind, soft as dust; the dropped twigs lie.
The obdurate trunks keep, sandstone-red,
A bloom, a shade of shade of sky
Darkening. Alone here I should be afraid.

68

Alone here I should be afraid.
You are my innocence. Alone I should
Sink under hauntings I'd encounter here
Or bring here. Now they give the wood
Only an edge on peace, an autumn frost of fear.

Times of Life

No longer the unbridled crying near or far
Of little children calls me – their archaic voices.
I know they are not mine – whose learned weeping presses
Like ours against a heavy door,

Who are not always near, in the lap, in the house's hollow,
In the cradle mind; but free among the circling flocks
Now write on field and street invisible their tracks,
Paths in the air of lark or swallow.

My thought dwells on those trails, picks out and silvers them.
But the cries of infants knock, and yet must house elsewhere –
From road or neighbouring garden filling a world of air
Like wail of lambs from a mountain stream.

Agnostic

I have lived my life long
With one who cannot speak a word,
Or if a word, not of my tongue
More than sound of stream or bird;
Or if of my tongue, unheard.

I am deaf or this is dumb,
This life and world apart from me
To whom betrothed at birth I came,
In whose silence most I see
A calling soul, calling my scrutiny.

So where deepest silence lies
Gathered to pools, my steps will draw:
The speechless child that sleeps or cries;
Age with the secret, not the power;
The look of utterance on the silent flower.

You with religious faith, to whom
Life speaks in words you understand –
Believe, I also with my dumb
Stranger have made a marriage bond
As strong and deep and torturing and fond.

A Distant View of Parnassus

So, it is true, they are not gentle,
The Muses, hardly if at all
Accessible. Their mountain wall
Offers no hold to root or tendril.
Seeds of pansies, rock rose, even
Parnassus grass might strike and fall
From cliffs so gaunt, high, virginal,
So harsh to earth, so locked with heaven.

A Dream Forgotten

As I woke from a harrowing dream,
Fifty years old in me the habit of waking said:
"Loosen it; it is a dream.
Open your hand; you need not unwind the coils in the thread.
The lost need not be found, the truth need not be told.
Release your hold."

So as the waker must
I did, and out of sleep fell into dreamless waking.
That iron fabric passed
Frail out of mind as foam on sand, the clear domes breaking;
Faster than sound or light, faster than anything known,
Covering its tracks, was gone.

With relief on a cool
Shore stranded, yet I strained towards the dark where the harsh
    dream went.
It was a world and full
As any world of sorrow, fear, bewilderment.
Yet it bore life, and interest was its circling breeze,
And pearls enhanced its seas.

If to die should be so –
To hear: "It is a dream; let it go" and loose as we must
The unknown that's all we know –
Even in oblivion I should mourn a whole world lost.
Signs dark to understand, pearls never dived for yet
I should find means to regret.

VI
Translations from the Italian of
Giovanni Pascoli (1855-1912)

They are Ploughing

In the morning fields, where fiery red a spray
Of vine still burns in the hedge-row, and from bushes
The early mist like smoke is flowing away,

They are ploughing: one man urging on the slow
Cattle, slow-voiced, one sowing, one who pushes
The clods of earth back with his patient hoe.

And all they do the knowing sparrow watches,
Feasting in fancy, from its bramble hold,
And the robin sees, and out of woods and hedges
Sends its slight tinkling song that shines like gold.

Romagna
(To Severino)

Always one village, always, haunting me,
One inward landscape smiles, or mourns, Severino.
However far you journey there, you see
Still the blue phantom peak of San Marino.

This is my countryside, where the Malatesta
And Guidi reigned, and with his desperadoes
The bold and gentle Ferryman was master,
King of the highroads and the forest shadows.

There in the stubble where the turkey hen
Goes sobbing with her foster brood, by the glittering
Light on the pool and the scattered water when
The slow ducks with their rainbow heads are weltering –

Oh, if we could be there, lost in green cover!
Or standing by the elms, the nest of the jay,
Could shout and hear our voices, carried over
The mid-day drowsing farms, die far away,

75

Where the bent labourer raises his head
And lays his sickle down and lifts his bowl,
And the tired cattle dream in peace and shade,
Munching their sainfoin in the dusk of the stall;

And from far villages we'd hear the bell –
Tower beyond tower, that with their silver cries
Call to cool shelter, call to quiet, call
To where the table flowers with children's eyes.

Once, at my home, an acacia tree would spread us
Its lacy sunshade for these scorching hours.
All summer long it gave its leaves to shade us
And filled our eyes with its rosy feathered flowers;

And close beside it, by the crumbling wall,
Thick-set and dense with leaves a rose tree held
A jasmine in its arms, and over all
A poplar chattered like a noisy child.

This was my nest, and dreaming there I rode
With Guidon Selvaggio or Astolfo far
Across the hills; or there before me stood,
Pale in his Hermitage, the Emperor.

And while I fought with heroes, while I soared
High with the Hippogriff in dreams of glory,
Or in the silence of my room I heard
Exiled Napoleon dictate his story,

I would hear through all, where the hay lay freshly mown,
The crickets' song perpetually quiver,
And from their brooks I would hear the frogs intone
Their wordless poem that goes on for ever.

And long and endless poems without words,
Foreshadowings and dreams of poems, came to me:
Rustle of summer leaves, piping of birds,
Laughter of women, roaring of the sea.

This was our nest; but on a bitter day
We flew, late swallows, from the home of our birth.
My country now is where I live, but they
Had not so far to go; they were laid in the earth.

So I shall never come again through your hazy
Mornings, your dusty hawthorn lanes, to where
My nest lay deep in leaves – for fear the lazy
Cuckoo has come and left her fledgelings there –

My loved Romagna, where the Malatesta
And Guidi reigned, and with his desperadoes
The bold and gentle Ferryman was master,
King of the highroads, king of the shadows.

The Hedge
(A section of a long poem about country people)

I

Hedge of my holding, faithful and benign,
Rounding this garden like the wedding ring
That names as mine the woman who is mine

(And I your husband proud and flourishing,
Gentle dark earth, ready to love and please
The tyrant with his burnished harrowing)

Hedge, keeping out with your intricacies
The daytime-drowsy thief, welcoming all
Nest-building birds and grazing swarms of bees;

Hedge I repaired and strengthened like a wall
As still the household grew – re-planted part,
Every day happier, richer not at all;

Of hawthorn, tamarisk and pomegranate
With honeysuckle scent flowing between:
Through you I am rich and lord of my estate,

Hedge of my holding, city-wall of green.

II

How wise you are! – If thirsty travellers
Come by you offer berries for their pleasure,
But save the fruit-trees with their dangling pears.

You bring no gifts towards the housewife's treasure,
Her hoarded jars; but happy in your care
She reaps the laden cherry-trees at leisure.

You bring no gifts, and yet the vines declare
(When by the track I prune them, and the voice
Of the cuckoo from the hill is in the air) –

Declare: "You are our father; as you choose
You rule, and guide us through the poplar maze.
But the hedge is the mother who takes care of us."

"Through her I have oil and wine for all my days"
I answer. From the yard the cocks call too,
Applauding, and the watch-dog barks his praise –

Who is a voice, my silent hedge, to you.

III

And yet you do speak briefly in your turn,
Mute at the boundary, giving the world
A prohibition sharper than a thorn;

Giving consent, like flowers, within the fold;
Hedge firm to others, but to me benign,
Like the faith given with a ring of gold

That names as mine the woman who is mine.

The Kite

There is something new today in the bright air,
New and yet old. I am in a different mood
And place, and smell the violets in flower.

They are in flower in the monastery wood,
In the Capuchins' school, under the brown
Of leaves the wind stirs at the oak-tree's foot.

And the air, sweet to breathe, is breaking down
The hardened clods of earth and visiting
Countryside churches with their steps grass-grown;

An air of a different place, a different spring,
A different life from this; a sky-blue air
That holds a flock of white shapes hovering –

Our kites are up, yes, soaring high and far.
For this is a holiday. We trooped between
Hedges of blackberry and hawthorn here.

The hedges all were spined and bare; no green,
But here and there a few of autumn's red
Berries in clusters, or a white flower shone

Of spring. A robin hopped and pivoted
On a bare branch; a lizard through the dry
Leaves in the ditch poked up its little head.

And this is where we stop, in sight of high
Windy Urbino – all of us now vying
To launch our comets on the turquoise sky.

There it goes, wavering, colliding, dying –
And lifts, and takes the wind. Oh, there at last,
Through the long yell from the throats of the boys, it is flying.

Flying; from our hands snatching its string so fast,
It seems a flower in flight on its thin stem,
Escaped to flower again on another coast.

Flying; and the breathless lungs and face aflame
And trembling legs of the child, and heart, and eyes –
Into the sky it is sweeping all of them.

Higher, still higher! A bright dot, it flies
So high, a shining spark. Oh, but a wind
Sidelong, a cry...Whose voice is it that cries?

I know them all, the voices of that band;
Strange how across the years I know them well,
One sweet, one shrill, one muffled and low-toned.

And one by one again I see you all,
My school-friends; and you with them, you whose white
Face on a shoulder drooping lay so still.

I said the prayers over you, at night
I cried for you. Yet you were happiest.
The wind brought down for you only a kite.

It is your whiteness I remember best,
And how your knees kept still a trace of red
From our long praying where the floor had pressed.

Oh, you were happiest, who went to bed
Clasping your favourite toy, and closed your eyes
And followed easily where you were led.

For death is surely kind to one who dies
Clasping his childhood, as a flower unblown
Keeps folded its white petals where it lies

Cut off in bud. Oh, dead in childhood, soon
I shall be coming too under the earth
Where you have slept in peace so long alone.

Better to come there rosy, out of breath
And warm with sweat – straight from the open air
And the race to the hill-top, better to come to death.

Better to come there with your head still fair.
For you, when you lay cold upon the sheet,
It was your mother combed your wavy hair,

Gently so that you were not hurt by it.

The Servant Girl from the Mountains

All of them out, all of them gone.
Timid and wild, the girl from the hills
Left in the kitchen sits alone.
The copper pans hang on the walls.
Her eyes roam all about her, then
Fall to her lap again.

Nothing familiar round,
Nothing she knows; all dark and dumb
Looms to her sight. And not a sound
But when the flies on the window hum;
But for the low and inward clucking
The pot on the fire is making.

A sharp mouse-muzzle comes·
And goes at a crack, and comes once more.
The water heating on the flames
Changes its note and rings...From far,
Farther away than heart can tell
The sound falls of a bell...

Of a mule on the mountain track –
Higher and higher, on and on
Between the distant small and black
Beech-trees climbing, seen and gone;
Only the swaying bell at its neck
Sounds on without a break.

Still an hour of day to come.
In the blue air the moon is a flake.
How lovely to be journeying home
Through the long evening, still not dark.
One of those days that never end,
And the scents of summer round.

The far-off singing bell
Is almost lost in all she hears;
Lost in the mountain waterfall
There at her feet, filling her ears,
And in the constant changing breeze
Through the full leaves of the trees.

She hears the nightingale
Singing, now other birds are dumb,
Alone, alone but for the owl,
Tuning for her watch to come,
That will end when morning breaks
At the chiming of the larks.

The Sound of the Pipes

*(In Advent, shepherds came down from the hills before dawn and played
a traditional tune before shrines of the Virgin.)*

I heard in my sleep the pipers tuning.
I heard their lullay an hour before morning.
Through all the sky the stars are shining.
In all the cottages lights are burning.

The shepherds have come so far from the darkened
Folds of their mountains down to us here.
Behind the cottage walls they have wakened
All the good people, simple and poor.

Now under the beam they light the wick –
All of them yawning, heavy from bed.
Those lights are laden with sleep and dark
And hush of talking and weight of tread.

Those votive lanterns everywhere burning,
Here at the window, there by the wall,
Have made of the world, an hour before morning,
A candle-lit crib as vast as small.

The stars through all the dark sky shining
Seem stilled to listen from far in space;
And now in the valley the pipes, beginning,
Lift up their melting voices of peace:

Voices of peace in church or cell,
Voices of home and the children sleeping,
The mother singing; voices of all
Our lost, assuaging, causeless weeping.

O pipers, come from the years before
The day, before reality:
Now while the stars are bright in the air
Watching our transient mystery,

While no-one yet has laid the meal,
While no-one yet has lit the fire,
Before the bells begin to peal,
Give us your leave to weep an hour.

Not now without a cause, with a host
Of causes; yes; but the heart demands
That flood of crying that then is past,
That storm of sorrow that breaks and ends.

Still it desires that innocent rain
Over its new, real torments and fears;
Over its pleasure, over its pain
Prays for those far-off reasonless tears.

The Weaver

I come to the bench in front of the loom,
Just as I used to in years out of mind.
She, as she used to, moves to make room
In front of the loom.
And never a sound, no word at all.
Only her smile comes, gentle and kind.
Her white hand lets the shuttle fall.

With tears I ask: How could I have gone?
How could I have left you, my long-desired?
Silent she answers with tears alone:
How could you have gone?
And draws towards her, sadly and slow,
The silent comb; and never a word.
Silent the shuttle flies to and fro.

With tears I ask: Why does it not sing,
The treble comb, as it did long ago?
Gentle she echoes me, wondering:
Why does it not sing?
And: O my love – says, weeping, weeping –
Have they not told you? Do you not know?
I have no life now but in your keeping.

Dead, I am dead, yes; weaving, I weave
In your heart only. So it must be
Till wrapped in this sheet at last, my love,
I sleep by you, near the cypress tree.

Night-Flowering Jasmine

And the flowers of night unfold in the hour
When I remember those
I love. And moths of dusk appear
In the heart of the guelder rose.

An end has come to calls and songs;
Only one house hums on.
The nests are sleeping under wings
As eyes under their lids drawn down.

Out of the open cups of the flowers
Their strawberry scent is shed.
The light shines in the wakeful house.
The grass springs on graves of the dead.

By the full hive loiterers buzz,
Late stragglers at the door.
The Hen leads out her brood of stars
Over the dark-blue threshing-floor.

All night the scent wells from the flowers
And the wind scatters it.
The lamp is carried up the stairs,
Shines at a window and goes out.

And morning comes; the flowers fold.
The crumpled petals brood,
Enclosed in their soft, secret world,
What strange and new beatitude?

The Woodmen's Friend

The foreign woodmen, slow to talk,
Have spread through all the forest near.
You hear the saw from dawn to dark,
Shi and *shi*, *shi* and *shi*.
Their home is in the mountains where
The day begins, beyond the sea.

In couples, one who stands upright,
The other facing, on his knees.
The kneeling man is bent and white,
The one who stands is the younger one.
What powerful arms among the trees
Move up and down, up and down!

Only the robin watches them,
Now from a branch, now from the ground.
It hops and flies from stone to stem
And twirls and flutters, tree to tree,
And sends its sweet refrain around
Between the sounds of *shi* and *shi*.

The Saint required a plumb-straight line
To mark his block of cypress wood.
Now Mary, suckling her Son,
Was in the house beside the fire,
But there at hand the robin stood.
Saint Joseph called to it: "Come here."

He dipped his sponge in dye, and red
He stained his string with sinopite.
"This end, take in your beak," he said.
"Stand here and hold it carefully."
Mary in her loved retreat
Missed the sound of *shi* and *shi*.

Now silent, he unwound the twine
From off its reel, along the beam,
And drew it back, stretched taut and fine,
Ready to rebound upon...
But through the air an "Ave" came:
There was Mary with her Son.

The bird flashed round, and all askew
The red string slipped and marked the beam.
The Saint snatched up his sponge and threw...
And stained its feathers. So we see
Why now the redbreast is its name.
And when it hears the *shi* and *shi*

It still will come between the boughs
To watch and flutter, watch and sing;
And though it will not come so close,
For it is wiser now than then,
Its song consoles their wandering,
Poor exiled tribe, the foreign men.

VII

Pain has its Innocence

Pain has its innocence: extremity
Of sorrow lends its own pure quality.
Freak tides that drown the soul awhile confer
A lustre that is theirs and not of her.
The ruined lands lie bare when deep floods fall;
Awhile now, crystal water covers all.

An Ordinary Autumn

Leaves dying and the light of autumn speak of death
And poetry. The light's hallucinatory calm
Though known for fragile seems eternal over earth;
And the leaves, as beloved and numberless as words,
Emptied of function, look towards their dying storm.

And yet it is an ordinary autumn, with the birds
Intent on the last pears fallen, and through holes in the net
Of summer more naked in their coming and going,
And the leaves' selves not miraculously bright
As some years, fallen to ashy fairness, or still showing

Their dark green, like experience worn. And still the light
Oblique and tempered is as wonderful as gold,
And the gold brush-strokes of the leaves of Solomon-seal
Sign the garden; all is common; I being old
(And that is common too) this year more dearly feel
The metaphor of autumn painted on the world.

In a Foreign Land

Dark is to me this forested country.
Sweet rustling words are hard to follow
And roots of nameless trees along the heart lie shallow.

But water is one the whole world over.
Not strange is light on any inland river
Nor strange, in the wide famous estuary for ever

The enormous tide, just as in any other,
On its open palm, in its candid power
Lifting the water-weed, the cradle leaf and flower.

The Sandy Yard

One day at noon I crossed
A sandy yard planted with citrus trees
Behind a small hotel. I walked slowly in the sun
With feet in the hot sand which the leaf-cutting ants
Crossed too, under their little sails of green, filing
Intent; and I thought, this
I will keep, I will register with time: I am here;
And always, shall have been here – that is the wonder –
Never, now, not have been here; for now I am here,
Crossing the sandy yard
Between the citrus trees, behind the small hotel.

The Expatriate Girl

From our land of spring
And autumn and cold seas and long
Shadows journeying
She has built her house among

92

The sharp simplicities:
The mountains and the royal sea,
The noonday shadowless trees,
And poverty, and gaiety.

Now she lays her head
On the volcanic beaches and
Her northern hair is spread
On their jet and crystal sand.

Winter Song

Between two ice ages
Before the shortest day,
Walking in the mild air
And on the yielding clay

And on the grassy tussocks
That fill their rifts and caves
As dark and bright as violet beds
With sodden drifted leaves,

Walking in the green winter
That has drunk the snow
We talk as sea-borne strangers would
When travelling was slow.
Spring is in doubt, a death ahead,
Summer, a life ago.

Alloway's Guides

He closed his book and told this tale to me,
I tell again for what I found it worth:
In love with space, in love with stringency
Alloway journeyed to the ends of the earth.

In the bloom of empire and exploration
He climbed unclimbed mountains and traversed ranges
Doubtfully mapped, and he crossed the central Asian
Desert, in love with extremity and strangeness.

There travelling with camels by night in the hot season
With three men (guides and servant) he watched the guides
Steer by the stars with infallible precision
Over a thousand miles immune to roads.

And once there trudging through gravelly sand beside
The camels, through days without landmarks like the plain,
He saw a man sprint ahead – the younger guide –
Grow small and vanish – and asked where he had gone.

"His home is here. No doubt he has gone home."
So they caught up with him by the poor tents,
Four in number, pitched by a trickle of stream
In the pure unkindness of soil and elements

At the ends of the earth; and he for his few pence,
The blithe serene young man, came on with them.
Alloway thought of the ranges of experience,
And envied him, and fell to dreams of home.

The Geese on the Park Water

1

The Canada geese
Pose in the light and dark of ripples,
And in and out of narrow shadows
Pose, compose, improvising
Their endless eloquent line.

94

And elongated, dissolved by ripples,
Cast by the trees, tree-casts, the shadows
Are only material for the posing,
Are driftwood salvaged for the composing,
The endless flow-away improvising
Of the Canada geese.

2

Like the arts that exist in time
Alone or essentially –
Acting, dancing, even
Music and poetry –
The lives of men and of birds,
The line their living scores
Upon time, the notes or words
Are as if performed. But for whom?

For us the dancing; the elegant
Water-birds if they pose
These do not pose for us
Though their existence flows
Away in forms that to us
Are grace, grace flowing out
Like water wasted in drought
Constantly into unbeing.

Time is a sluice set open
And through it, we mourn, too fast
All beauty shown or spoken,
Apprehended, runs to the past.
Yet what quells my mind the most
Is not the loved and known
But the unregarded un-
Apprehended constantly flowing,

Unless there is God, to waste;
As, when the gates close, unseen,
Unknown (as we think of knowing)
The Canada geese on the lake

Will transpose from now to the past
(For now, while we say it, is past)
Will compose for time and death
(For time is promised to death)

Their endless eloquent line.

The Unused Morning

On a long column scarcely fluted
The early daylight lifts its day's hours,
And in our garden the southern hemisphere's
Lilies on their long columns raise
Through individual silences,
Beyond the curtain, spires of fine-drawn flowers

Like southern stars, like and unlike
Our own lilies, our imprinted constellations.
But I, how long now have I been awake
Or in and out of sleep, a seagull skimming
Its lifted waves; a loafer dreaming
In doorways of a constant summer region?

In summer or a summer land,
Idling from in to out-of-doors, returning,
Is a light drifting between open rooms.
All thresholds dissipate; the dust enters and
The warm air like a house-dog goes and comes –
As we through sleep in the unused morning.

Two Visits to a Hillside

The children from overseas are on the chalk hill
Picking the almost stemless flowers: small
Among the whitening flints gentian, hawkweed
And flowers too many and obscure to tell.
The little girl says, "Girls pick flowers to smell them,
Boys pick them to mash them." But if we say
We like the flowers without a word they lay
Each at our feet a doll's-house-sized bouquet,
Smile and are gone for other flowers to swell them.

And later, lower down, where stones out-star
All gold and blood-drop flowers – treating rough ground
And thorned shrubs carefully, prospecting there
Alone and self-contained, the boy has found
An island continent of blackberries,
Australia of strange fruits, and brings to us
A palmful of specimens; and we say yes,
Eat some and keep us some; and so he does,
So both do, dark on the white galaxies.

That was late summer; now the year is failing.
The children have gone home across the ocean.
Here are a few blackberries, soggy in the trailing
Vague sweet autumn, and brown spikelets of gentian.
And still the slope with its stone immortelles
Is dyed with dark and small intensities
Where the children played (as a light or window is
Found printed under eyelids when they close);
Still printed with his bearing, with her songbird calls.

The Cross-Country Journey

Seen by the passenger, the further the range
The slowlier it will change (yet it will change)
But what is near beyond the window-ledges,
Half seen, is gone: the cattle by the hedges,
The section of canal, the beaten lanes,
The children in their faithful love of trains
Waving from fences, hanging over bridges.

So we in our slow lives – for they seem slow,
Though what can we compare with all we know? –
Journeying cross-country watch the loved and near
Run by, till dazzled we rest eyes on the far,
On the abstract hills, on the unresponding
Beauty of earth, or the sun let down to a landing
Or entering rooms where the drifts of memory are.

The foreground flashes on – there by the willows
They are bathing now, as we were in the shallows
Of middle age lately or long ago –
While still the hills maintain the journey slow,
Accompanying us as after dark the moon might,
As now the sun... yet the slant itself of the sunlight
Assents to change, with all the world we know.

To an Infant Grandchild

Dear Katherine, your future
Can never meet my past.
So short our common frontier,
Our hinterlands so vast.

Yet at the customs post
Light airs pass freely over
And all we need to know
We know of one another.

Though day will wake your country
As dark flows over mine
Your outback sleeps in shadow now.
Your smile is cloudless dawn.

Strollers in a Park

1

One thing was new in the much visited park,
In the cooling air, day turning early towards dark,
On the stone bridge over the man-made width of the lake.

They were grazing sheep in the park; it was this was unwonted.
Thirty . . . a hundred . . . two hundred say, he counted
And reckoned, crossing the bridge unattended,

Jostling, accommodating, as the sand
Streams in an hour-glass, from the green broads beyond
To out-fan again over the near-side ground.

"I have never seen so many pressing through
Field gates or straying on fells," she said; "it is true
Always, lacing the old we meet the new."

They took the bridge after the last stragglers
Had crossed and the lame ones and the unambitious
Were cropping the sweet home grass among the others

In patriarchal calm spread far and wide
Between the great façade and the waterside,
Now nonchalant and satisfied.

2

The lake draws in for the bridge, and on both sides
Spreads (as the sheep flock narrowed and now spreads)
As far each way as beauty alone decides.

Below the bridge, on every shelf of its piers
Domestic pigeons settle and converse,
Whose murmuring cannot but seem love's to us.

The strollers paused in mute community
By one then the other parapet. Each way
Water and land had been changed to please the eye,

Yet seemed – because the artist had judged well
And because light is powerful over all –
Under the clouded sun seemed natural.

And we are nature's, and our seeing is
A part, she thought, also a part of this.
The silver stretches were infinities.

"We have come here many times; we shall not come
As many more." "But some," he said; "but some."
They watched through glasses before turning home

Mallard and coot on the darker water, made
So dark by the further trees' shelter and shade.
"And we have seen today's new thing," she said.

A Photograph from Abroad

The dark child in her darker than sky-blue dress,
Tall, pliant, pretty, seven or eight years old –
Posed for her photograph to bend and hold
One of the stems (as obediently she does)
Of the plant that patterns the verandah's view –
The child on the lacy verandah and the tropical
Pennon-leaved shrub straying over sky and all,
They make a design that might be a poem too.

And so I wrote to her mother. What, though, seeing
That in the way of mysterious light expression
Of a small beauty, all is done, what are words to
Express or be? What is the poem to do?
Nothing to do but follow its vocation.
Nothing to be but tribute to what is in being.

The Pensioner

At the time of morning when the recesses
In bedroom walls stand forward like tall ghosts,
And as curtains thin, the fine wings of the swarms
That flecked the dark catch a softer and generalised light,
And furniture takes up its being and weight,
And it is our world again whose nightly dissolved
White foam is again overriding the dark of its sea:

At such a time of day in early or late
Winter the pensioner, old man or woman
Cast up on morning, may forebode the cold,
And foresee beyond the eastward curtains, beyond
The shrubs and roof-tops, those now leafless trees,
Those shapes of poplars whose beauty even more
Than on the sky is imprinted on his days.

And he may think the sky will be beautiful
As well, with sunrise fantasies – or plain,
Neutral or rainy, no matter; the birds may at
The drawing of curtains explode, though softly, away
From their bare twigs or chosen evergreens,
But he will have seen them, starlings, chaffinches,
Perhaps a thrush; domestic as their names.

And he may foretell going down through the muted cold
Of the house, filling the kettle, making tea,
And feel the deed adventurous, something done
A first or last time (as fragility
And strangeness cast their colours); and foretaste
The warmth of the tea; and may go to meet the familiar,
Adhering to it, knowing beyond thought it is not for ever.

101

The Young Couple

So this young couple came to see me – why
I have forgotten, and what their names might be.
I did not know them, but as if long known
I more than liked, I loved them. We sat down
Awhile. Perhaps they had come with some idea
Of buying the house, for we wandered here and there.
She said, "The spare-room?" "At the turn of the stair."
She came back saying, "I cannot find a door."
I went with her; there was no room at all
At the turn of the stair. There was a papered wall
And a window on the garden, as before
The house was altered, long before our time.
So then I understood. I said, "My dear,
We are figures in a dream." I said to them
"Perhaps it is your dream," for pity's sake,
"And you will wake." I thought they would not wake.
I kissed their fading lips that never spoke
Again, who had been my friends. And so I woke.

In the Basement Room

In the window of the room, in our cave's adit,
Between falls of the vine and the lichen-green acrylic,
We keep each year a vase of that year's papery
Seeds, the Americans with more simplicity
Call Silver Dollars, we
As if from long experience call Honesty.

Shadowy, spotted, nacreous, not silver, less than white...
Loved by the light: only for them the last of light
Enters the basement room, slipped through the pavement's bars,
By the streaked and ferny area wall, through the window glass
To the seeds in their cold vase –
Pervious or light-reflecting, never not luminous.

A million years ago we brought the flawed and pearled
Gift of our honesty to the thousand million of our world's
By mind neglected garden: we brought our consciousness,
Such as it is; if silver, tarnished; fatal – none the less
No yard of earth but has
Been dwelt upon by us, been loved by some of us.

If I held any creed, at this time I would pray
To whatever light might mean in my faith's imagery:
"Do not forsake us now. Such as we are, we are
– Translucent or reflecting – your best lovers here;
We only, apt for incandescence when you come
To your neglected garden, to your basement room."

A Beach in the Antilles

In the late afternoon the sun in fast decline
Still struck from the sands of ash their pewter shine.
The light-boned children still played on the water-line.

Three women all the day had watched or swum,
And talked, and served the meal when it was time.
In the late afternoon there fell on them,

Over and round them, a slow snow of white
Flowers, flowers fallen not blown, in light
Showers or singly from the moderate height

Of the wooded cliff. None of us knew the name
Of the flowers nor knew, as slowly we noticed them,
From which tall tree, sprawled up the cliff, they came;

But they came to rest, a few at first on the sand
As if they had grown there, then over the strewn ground
On a cast shoe, in a drained cup, on a hand,

On a net or a shell: trumpet flowers, candle white.
And if they had been butterflies, as by their flight
They almost seemed, they could give no more delight,

Signing the day's perfection so, at the fall of night.

The Dead

The dead are music, the dead are poetry.
The hero dead is a ballad, the child dead is a song,
A rounded water-drop, seamless, a few lines long,
And the first and the last lines are the same

So that it can be sung on and on.
The living are told in verbs, the dead is a noun alone.
The living are prose, and with prose what varied things can be
    done!
But the dead is a poem: the poem is solely a name.

The Evening Garden

Not dark nor light but clear,
But lucid with no source of light,
But breathing with no flow of air
The garden journeys into night.

Late gangling flowers lean –
Anemones, tobacco flowers –
Over the gravel, over the brown
And silken leaves that mulch the grass.

More than I did, I now
Leave in this lighted room undrawn
The curtains. More than it used to do
The garden presses on the pane,

Or seems it does, in this
One hour when all is seeming, when
It wars with shadowy lights in the glass,
And losing, is most potent then –

Only in this one hour,
Tidal, returns – day's utmost edge –
Pressing with eyes of question or power,
Gold wild-cat eyes on the window-ledge.

Walled plot of fruit-trees, flowers,
What strength it wields, how hard it bears!
Why should it not bear hard? It has
Behind it all the universe.

The lighted room is small.
Now we exist; and now we fashion
A garden and a girdling wall,
Our salient into wild creation.

The Space Between

From this high window best, you see the briar rose
In its short flowering – how the yellow one has spread
Rangy above the white on the deep-sea garden bed;
As clouds lie over clouds in archipelagos,
But small as petals on the grass, under the wing
Of the soaring plane. And are they clouds or can they be,
Those deepest down, foam flecks or mountain waves of sea?
Our eyes are dazed by nature's see-through curtaining,

Layer upon layer stretched, woven to all degrees
Of part-transparency: the rose, knotted like lace
To a star pattern, thins between to stellar space.
Though eyes before they learn level the galaxies,
It is not the flowers' selves only, webbed in their skies of green,
It is depth they grant to sight; it is the space between.

VIII

The Scent

She had forgotten, talking, in her hand
Were roses. Otherwise how could it be
Their scent had come upon her unawares
And seemed a stray from thought or memory,
A shoot or spring of deepest clear content
Breaking out from the dark ground of the mind,
Before she understood the scent was theirs,
Before she recognised it as a scent?
As happiness can meet one waked from sleep
And not at first bring back to mind its cause
And close its wings of light upon its small
And mortal bones and take its given shape,
So that bliss hung, before it claimed it was
Her roses' scent, or had a name at all.

Images of Age

The sluggish changes that are not seen till done,
The palace revolutions out of the blue,
When they come true seem long to have been true.
I have heard, where the Negro meets the Amazon

And black transparent and white waters join
(The white opaque with silt, emulsified)
A stretch, unmixed, the two flow side by side
Till the white overwhelms. Age must come on,

When sleep invading blood in the veins moves.
Then dreams are narrow runnels under moss,
Almost, barely, the moor grass meets across –
Blue of the sky on its strawy lacing leaves.

The Confidence

So she told her Greek story
Facing the daylight window,
Her gull-grey eyes opaque
And swept of shadow:
Monstrous, grievous, heroic,
Like something legendary
Yet not to be re-told
Till the end of the world.

Massive as kings' tombs,
Secret as graves grassed over,
Larger than life though life
Is large, this grief.
Friend, brave enough, not braver
But equal to what comes,
The words that would be tender
Are lost in wonder.

Listening to Collared Doves

I am homesick now for middle age, as then
For youth. For youth is our home-land: we were born
And lived there long, though afterwards moved on
From state to state, too slowly acclimatising
Perhaps and never fluent, through the surprising
Countries, in any languages but one.

This mourning now for middle age, no more
For youth, confirms me old as not before.
Age rounds the world, they say, to childhood's far
Archaic shores; it may be so at last.
But what now (strength apart) I miss the most
Is time unseen like air, since everywhere.

And yet, when in the months and in the skies
That were the cuckoos', and in the nearer trees
That were the deep-voiced wood-pigeons', it is
Instead now the collared doves that call and call
(Their three flat notes growing traditional),
I think we live long enough, listening to these.

I draw my line out from their simple curve
And say, our natural span may be enough;
And think of one I knew and her long life;
And how the climate changed and how the sign-
Posts changed, defaced, from her Victorian
Childhood and youth, through our century of grief;

And how she adapted as she could, not one
By nature adaptable, bred puritan
(Though quick to be pleased and having still her own
Lightness of heart). She died twenty years ago,
Aged, of life – it seems, all she could do
Having done, all the change that she could know having known.

Bright Margins

I thought of decoration, such as once was done
To frame a manuscript – how the finished work is one,
Cornflowers and gold are one with the marmoreal
Script, with the firm and sounding Latin words as well
And the meaning of the words – no meaning but a bell

Whose overtones dissolve its note that would be clear;
And thought again – in the wide borders of the year
Walking by blue and golden flowers and like the moon
Self-shadowed white, short-lived in autumn garden beds
That are bright margins too – how they seem the silk of threads,
Not woven in the cloth, embroideries, not the words
Nor the meaning of the words; and still the work is one.

Seeing the Baby

Far down he seems to sleep on the ground of a pool
Trees overcast or a deep well.
Yet the water is clear; the shadow-colour thrown
On the white sheet is all his own,
The tender sallow that is warm as cool.

You lend me your child, so nearly new, to see.
If I should touch him it would be
A different thing, but the long shaft of sight
Isolates as a field-glass might,
And the deep walls of the cradle simplify.

He could not be smaller and still human. Flowers
Encapsulate a world for us.
Jewels pack large in small, of beauty, cost,
Strangeness. Of all on earth, he most
Most stores in little substance: human, ours.

At the Gate of the Junior School

Here is the gate with the young parents waiting there –
Some of them beautiful but not, as once they were,
As flowers are beautiful, no longer in that way.
Their used and hardy beauties are in fruit today.

Life for its reasons has them in its exigent employ –
Talking their in-group talk, watching for girl or boy.
And the children come, flickering like flames over cindery
    ground.
Each, they reclaim their own. Life has them in its hand.

112

The Long Grass

Our love was deep in the long grass
As clover flowers – not deeper was.
Not deeper are the ocean beds.
It was all that earth needs.

IX

The Hands of the Blind

As we are conscious of the hands of the blind
So learned with a different lore from ours,
Seeing the fingers like movements of a mind –
Slightly recurved, the distal phalanges
With their silk touch reading the universe;

Or as we may surprise on a blind face
The transit of a smile, like that on a young
Baby's alone, private, protectionless,
And sense another world, a silver one,
A moon before our landings on the moon;

And may in our complementary blindness grope
To touch pure nescience of sight, that bears
Gifts such as only choose its mode and scope –
In the fenced garden its particular flowers –
So I believe, of worlds further from ours,

To minds, not eyes, born dark, there must open vistas,
Lights burn in savage hearts. In tropical
Forests strange flowers, beaked heliconias
Amaze; on utmost snow sky colours fall –
Blindnesses, visions, being the gifts of us all.

A Portrait of a Boy

He frowns a little, facing the light.
The large leaves' shadows blot and camouflage
Him, laurel-shaped leaves and broad wings of poinsettia.

He has folded his arms, being eleven,
A proud age, and looks forward wholly directly
Out of the shadows, though he frowns a little

As if the light and the open prospect
Were adulthood, and he considering it
With all his attention, mustering all he can

117

Out of his leaf-pied childhood; and further
As if he were Man emergent from the forest
Of animal nature; Adam confronting his fate –

Knowledge, the shelterless light-washed spaces
Spread for him on and on – and bringing to bear
Consciousness: his integrity, all that he has.

The Fish in the Evenlode

That there is so much more than this
I know; and yet there is
That dark and stubborn fish that stays
Below the stream's engaging surface ways
And might be dozing in a sluggish dream
Yet keeps its place against the stream, headed upstream.

Like hair alive in water, here gilded on green
The long combed weeds flow and within
The shiftings of their flow the fish is seen, unseen.

And here in summer
White flowers of crowfoot will star over
The penetrable dusk of the small river,
Fairer than if some artist in Japan
Had touched them in faultlessly one by one
For nothing but delight, on his dark folding screen.

And still, moving nor moved, the fish lies low.
Its strength is equal to the water's flow.
Its name I surely know –
Self-will, the body's will; older than birth,
The creature's will (unwilled) to be and thrive on earth.

A Past Generation

The people who were old when we were young,
Then this is where they were; who made no song
Of trials or sorrows, having still our nation's
Historic phlegm, having their generation's
Reserve, or call it their civility,
That would not hurt or embarrass needlessly:
The people who grew weak as we grew strong,
The old when we were young.

A Woman Condemned to Virtue

From future time the grey flowed into her hair
As the light flowed into her mirror from outer space.
She looked in the mirror and saw her mother there.

"It is only a trick of light, the snow in the air...
But how shall I live my life, wearing her face?"
From future time the grey flowed into her hair

While antique voices chimed how alike they were,
For words half heard may find their time and place:
She looked in the mirror and saw her mother there.

"But she stays home-bound, gentle and wise in her chair,
And I am the wild one that runs a dangerous race."
From future time the grey flowed into her hair,

And the impartial winter light laid bare
In the bones of her skull a genetic calm and grace.
She looked in the mirror and saw her mother there.

We range less far than we think and from anywhere
May round the world to a long relinquished base.
From future time the grey flowed into her hair:
She looked in the mirror and saw her mother there.

A Present of Sea Shells

The shells are elaborate and curious
Like human thought, and yet not thoughts of ours.
A young boy searched them out on an island's shores
Where shells so perfect are not plentiful,
And in a carton, wrapped in cotton wool,
Sent them through air across the world to us,

Knowing that, settled far inland, we still
Love the sea's gifts, complex and beautiful.
This fact, this node of facts, in thought (like a shell
In the hand) I hold – the boy on the shore, the sun
On the wings of the mind-powered great machine homing in.
Time yields its patterned shells, none, none identical.

Waking in dark on the flat-lands of the night
To sadness, or space too vast, I light this light:
The boy designing our pleasure; and now, spread out
On a tray, the shells from their journeying. One is a dawn that
    pales,
One etched with finest fans on lapping scales,
One whorled; orange and green seem hand-strewn over it.

The Old Woman's Dream

She drowsed by day, being old: reality
Flowed into dream. And voices from nearby
Lawns, or of children loitering to play
On their route from the pool, these real voices came
Through the window and inhabited her dream.

For all that she knew clearly where she was
In her light sleep, still she wondered: are they ours –
Children's tones being so much alike – are those
Our children's voices? And her dreaming told
Her falsely, yes. A boy, say seven years old,

Come in by the glass door, sat briefly with her
And left, and came again with a girl. Together
In changing play they took one part and another –
Always her children. Nothing anywhere
Could be more natural than their being there.

Waking, she heard their voices ebb and drain
To those generic children in the lane
As colonists might be called home again;
And wondered, in the land from which they'd gone,
With what strange power the past claims to live on.

Three Poems in Memory of a Child

AN EARLY DEATH

Judith, my grandchild, older than I in death,
More learned in death than all the living, all
My parents' strong viable children, their
Children, and theirs: now in this seeming lull,
In the still, radiant autumn of this year,
Thinking of death, I think of you the more.

Love, I remember you twenty months old,
No toddler as a blonde child would have been –
A little girl, light running, a gazelle,
And gentle. I have not seen you since at all,
The Atlantic Ocean first, then death, between.
Of your long years you lived another one.

I called you learned in death more than us all,
Yet death you never knew in life, too young
Even to have heard its name, too quickly gone
For fear or pain to touch you, light gazelle.
And if the dead know death we cannot tell.
If in some way, in that way you know all.

And if in now way . . . yet to have been,
To have stood in the doorway in your shift of grace
With hands half lifted, so to have looked in
On mortal life, it is not nothing – is
A hammer stroke that rings and rings. Love, being
And not being both are strange; you belong to being.

THE NEW HOUSE

The new unfinished house
Had an emptiness, notwithstanding
The dusty garden soil
Brought in on feet or with winding
Of air through the window louvres,
And the florid heat abounding,
And the bell voices of children
Constantly sounding
Sweetly now, now clanging
Untimed; and with coming and going
The doors in the gusts banging.

The new inchoate house
Which the present and future filled
Had an emptiness, that held
The absence of the child,
The quiet one, never here.
And pain, unreconciled,
Drifting like air, dishevelled
The furnishing, and like stirring
Of earth had cracked the flooring:
Pain that can fracture the ground
Of a life beyond all curing.

This was before they had roofed
And walled with a lacy low
Parapet the verandah,
And planted quick to grow
Hibiscus, passion fruit,
And reclaimed the slope below
With pineapples and hardy

Root-crops and the rainfall tree.
This was while goats grazed free
Still over grass and thorns
And the litter of masonry.

But in those days, on the open
Verandah, work done, and cooled
The air and the thirsty land,
When the sun had dropped and the wild
Children had dropped like stones,
When they were still and were spread
Like wonders in shop windows
On the coverless sheet of the bed –
On the verandah, when light
From indoors fell soft as shade
And the voices of adults strayed,

Or the moon freed from the mountain
Poured equal light on the land,
The seaward fields and the sea's
Plains and long arc beyond –
On the sea and the unreclaimed
Land such quiet lay
As if the quiet child
Had taken her absence away;
Or as if the touch of the air
And the kindness of beauty and light
Had been news of her.

AN ISLAND GRAVEYARD

Wherever there are peopled islands there must be
Graveyards that overlook the sea.
They must be as numerous
As settled coasts; and the residuary grass
That snares our ankles will grow over
These wavy mounds and troughs everywhere, the survivor.

Where the brute innocent vegetation that the sun
One month cuts down the next is grown,
Here upon this young child's stone
Incised, the lettering straggles slightly, that was done
By an inexperienced hand, and this
Falls like a grace or truth, almost a happiness;

Calling to mind her child's inaptitudes, her starts
Of learning and her unlearned arts
And all her moving ways, both those
That other children share and those uniquely hers;
Saying, her nature's lettering, that we
Hold carved in us, is tooled as well on history

And stored in history's silence. Not eternal life
But having lived pleads to my unbelief
Its claim to everlastingness.
No foothold seems for thought, nor comfort much in this.
The past endures under what sun?
But, that she lived (our love knows) cannot be undone.

Here on this skyward field where she is not, but where
We easily can speak of her,
Where eyes are filled with sea and air
A few trees spread, always in leaf, now bright in flower.
But, island child, the sea was hers.
The sea she loved be a wreath for her, beyond words or flowers.

The Witness

Master of life, if our kind
Of life must come to an end,
I say this not in despair
Nor protest but as being
A witness, who was there
And knows what he is saying:
There is gold in the sand,
I have held it in my hand.

124

Here marvels past pretence
Unfold, and innocence
From valleys where it keeps
Is evidenced to us.
The child in the cradle sleeps
A petal on the grass.
New on the frozen tree
Leaves answer human dignity.

And since we came our lives
Have fed your cosmos, leaves
Falling. What do you do,
Master of time, with the past
That is seamed through and through
With our known and unexpressed?
Such a strange, so rich, compost
Have you in mind to waste?

If our world is your mistake
All said, it is yours to unmake,
To end as you began it.
We are more dark than bright
Yet faint from our perished planet
Quenched here, an obdurate light
Of meaning and of grace
Would travel still through space.

The Coach to the Airport

I think of living children, recalling that journey:
Out of all possible children, those few or many
Caught by chance in the net of our world and century;

How one had slept with her head on my lap, from having
Been wakened too early that day, the day of their leaving –
She slept in the coach to the airport while either side
Mist filled the morning fields, and the boy astride
The arm of the seat exclaimed at the blind white vision
And the red sun rising, four times magnified –

And how these are two of the few (though to us they are many)
Out of possible beings, caught in our delicate prison,
Wild natures caught in the net of our world and century.

Any Traveller's Apology

Part of my silence, part of my secrecy,
Was it a hard thing to ask you to be
Or the usual thing? This is obscure to me:
This clear: when in reality

Or fantasy I have been long away,
Say in the East or across the Ocean, say
Distant in work or mood from day to day,
Through being inescapably

The solitary traveller I am,
When I come home, to what but you do I come?
If you were gone I could never in fact or dream
Set out, for dread of coming home.

Water Images

THE TIDAL RIVER

The trees descend, image of love,
To drink the brackish water of
Estuary or tidal river,
To lean their inland fulness over
That bright and far-brought mineral other.

THE STREAM

So turbid though I am,
Rooted in me the young
Floated like water lilies –
That now alight like swans.

THE WELL

The stone you let fall in me will not resile
Nor echo nor give any sign awhile.
Wait for my word. A lifetime you may wait,
I am so deep, my depth so obdurate,
Not with my will but through my fate.

Reflecting on Old Age

We are as light as wood ash, dense as stone.
Our muscles come to know the weight of bone,
The sensual happiness of lying down.
A little milk the gradual years have pressed
Into our eyes that easily over-run.
Our vague hair is as volatile as dust.

Waking and sleep are mutual, so far on
In marriage that we speak of one alone,
Sleep without waking, as in a foreign tongue
Stumbling on consonants. Against the dark,
Coeval kindness, beneficence of the young
With our time's cares cross in a lattice-work.

Honey of small events, of passing states
We take – as when a light flame oscillates
In the smokeless coal. In the winter grate's
Rock garden it blows, translucent as a wild
Flower, as woodsorrel; or a bird's heart, it beats;
And gives peace, as if worlds were reconciled.

On the railway bank not only bracken, once,
I remember, but the dying grass was bronze
In transverse light; and beyond the journey, friends.
Happiness even passing imagination,
Foretold by straws of grass and bracken fronds,
Late in the day, their welcome at the station.

Too hard in age to trawl the heavy seas.
I settle for summations, instances,
Remembering (in time's interstices)
Time taken to sit in the tropic after-sun
In an open gallery, in hands cup or glass,
With two or three; here now, by a fire, with one.

X *New Poems*

Deaths of Flowers

I would if I could choose
Age and die outwards as a tulip does;
Not as this iris drawing in, in-coiling
Its complex strange taut inflorescence, willing
Itself a bud again – though all achieved is
No more than a clenched sadness,

The tears of gum not flowing.
I would choose the tulip's reckless way of going;
Whose petals answer light, altering by fractions
From closed to wide, from one through many perfections,
Till wrecked, flamboyant, strayed beyond recall,
Like flakes of fire they piecemeal fall.

Tree in Light Wind

Today the wind is human, it is tender.
If branches move, it is not altogether
But desultorily, one or another;
Tuning, like players in an orchestra,
One or another individually
His instrument before the symphony,
Head bent; but for its voice, solitary.

A Face in a Dream

Why do you undermine me so
With your conspirator's
Smile? We are not accomplices.
There is no secret guilt we share
But what is common as the air:
Guilt of not seeming all we are,
Not telling all we know.

You smile as children do who have lit
The fuse of some sweet joke
Laid to please though laid to shock.
But turn away your smile. I can
Even as it is hardly sustain
My light part in the play – so soon
I am to be awake
And have forgotten it.

The Stormy Child

He is two years old; he wakes from mid-day sleep
To plaintiveness that runs so fast to fury
The storm-pace dazzles. Are you hot, love, thirsty?
The cup crashes down. What is it he is saying?
(Slow to talk as if words were baulked at source.)
What is he saying in the eye of the hurricane,
Enclave of silence, what small timid word?
Saying 'I' and waiting for an answer?
Saying 'you' and listening for an echo?

Garden Weeds

Some years the common weeds,
Besides ground elder, were a small veronica
And yellow-flowered and silver-leaved archangel.
One year the wind or birds brought violet seeds
To land run wild of necessity a little:
Scentless dog violets, hedge violets – from where?

They were tribes on the move, such as come
Colonising, not marauding, spreading
Without volition as the sea's tide moves.
Where bare earth was between stems they filled the room
And flowered all summer, visible or hiding
The blue of their name in the equal green, the nap
    of their leaves.

They are childhood's flowers, or again
Bring their patina from another age, when earth's
Loved shell and poetry were seen as one;
Yet when this plot is brought to hand, will be gone,
Being weeds here and alien – as it may be, man
(Loved also, come from where?) is in the universe.

Old People

They dwell in sorrow. If a time may come
When they recall as happiness this time
Yet now they know that Sorrow is its name,

Their country of domicile; and that it is,
Like other countries, not without its flowers
(Although as insect-small as arabis,
Minutest crucifer in stones and grass) –

As when in nights strange and unselved with sleep
And waking, she goes down to bring him up
Chocolate in a cup or sweetened tea,
Emblem of better comfort than can be;
And thinks of midnight feasts that children scheme:
Closeness, adventure, waking dream.

The Paschal Moon

At four this April morning the Easter moon –
Some days to full, awkwardly made, yet of brazen
Beauty and power, near the north-west horizon
Among our death-white street lamps going down –
I wondered to see it from a lower storey
Netted in airy twigs; and thought, a fire
A mile off, or what or who? But going higher
I freed it (to my eyes) into its full glory,
Dominant, untouched by roofs, from this height seen
Unmeshed from budding trees; not silver-white
But brazed or golden. Our fluorescent light,
That can change to snow a moment of young green
In the maple tree, showed ashen, null and dead
Beside such strength, such presence as it had.